# Perfectly Me!

L. V. Zavala

Illustrated By: Dennis Davide

To order additional copies of this book, contact:
Xlibris
1-888-795-4274
www.Xlibris.com
Orders@Xlibris.com

To my son John, my special gift from God, who has always been just perfectly him.

Special thanks to my undying support, Cris, and to my creative support, Nadia Johnson.

Are you too short, or are you too tall?

I am just perfect, and that is all.

Are you too skinny, or are you too fat?

I am just perfect, and that is that.

Are you too silly, or are you too serious?

I am just perfect, since you are curious.

Is your nose too big? Are your eyes too small?

My face is just perfect, all in all.

Are your feet too long? Are your hands too wide?

I am just perfect, and so is my stride.

Do you talk too much? Or Are you too shy?

I am just perfect, and I'll tell you why.

I was created veeeeery carefully.

Much thought was given to what makes me unique

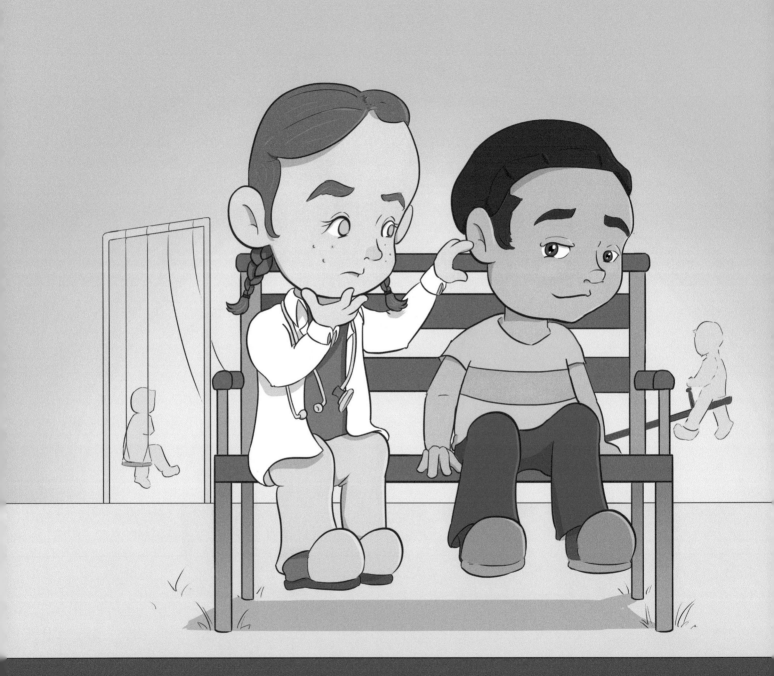

My eyes, my nose, my mouth, and my ears,

My joy, my sadness, my dreams, and my fears,

17

My knees, my feet, and my cute little toes,

My voice, my color, and the way my hair grows.

19

All were created with God's special touch.

And this is why God really loves me so much!

There's no one like me, not one will you find.

No one with my thoughts, no one with my mind.

I'm special.

I'm priceless.

I'm full of life and glee.

And you know what????

I am just perfectly me!

For the adults:

Greetings parents, caretakers, readers, and fellow armor bearers! This book carries a timely message for us. You and I live in a world where society tries its best to shape and mold our children into who it thinks our children should be. Following these trends too closely can lead to low self-esteem, depression, and other deviations in their mental, emotional, and spiritual well-being. It is up to us parents, family members, and other people who care, to invest in our children's security and in celebration of who they were created to be. Here are some tips to help you invest in the rejoicing of your children's identity.

1. Allow children to voice what they love about themselves. Help them focus on and feel good about features that cannot change, features which God uniquely created (skin color, features on the face, features on their bodies).

2. Promote feeling good about the uniqueness of how they were created. Talk about differences in features they may observe in other cultures they interact with. Foster an appreciation for God's creative artistry in themselves and in people they see every day.

3. Keep a journal to record all the wonderful things about your child that emerge as he or she grows. Periodically in their growing stages, they can look back and be reaffirmed in who they were designed to be.

4. Read and memorize scriptures and scriptural affirmations (encouraging statements formed from scriptural truths) that encourage your child in who they were created to be. Some samples are provided on the next page. However, please pray and read the scripture with your child. You will find that as your child spiritually matures, they will begin to point out scriptures that they can relate to themselves. They will learn how to employ these scriptures in their lives.

All scriptural references are taken from the NIrV Bible.

- "How you made me is amazing and wonderful. I praise you for that." (Psalm 139: 14)

- "God has loved me with an everlasting love." (Jeremiah 31:3)

- "God has made them [you can replace the word "them" with "me" to bring the Word closer to their hearts] a little lower than the angels. He placed on them a crown of glory and honor" (Psalm 8:5).

- "God saved me because He was pleased with me." (Psalm 18:19)

- "See what amazing love the Father has given us! Because of it, we are called children of God." (1 John 3:1)

- "The Lord my God is with me. He is the Mighty Warrior who saves. He will take great delight in me. In His love, He will sing for joy because of me. (Zephaniah 3:17)

Now you try!

Printed in the United States
By Bookmasters